FOOD LOVERS

ROASTS

FOOD LOVERS

ROASTS

RECIPES SELECTED BY JONNIE LÉGER

Trans
Atlantic
Press

All recipes serve four people, unless otherwise indicated.

For best results when cooking the recipes in this book, buy fresh ingredients and follow the instructions carefully. Make sure that everything is properly cooked through before serving, particularly any meat and shellfish, and note that as a general rule vulnerable groups such as the very young, elderly people, pregnant women, convalescents and anyone suffering from an illness should avoid dishes that contain raw or lightly cooked eggs.

For all recipes, quantities are given in standard U.S. cups and imperial measures, followed by the metric equivalent. Follow one set or the other, but not a mixture of both because conversions may not be exact. Standard spoon and cup measurements are level and are based on the following:

1 tsp. = 5 ml, 1 tbsp. = 15 ml, 1 cup = 250 ml / 8 fl oz.

Note that Australian standard tablespoons are 20 ml, so Australian readers should use 3 tsp. in place of 1 tbsp. when measuring small quantities.

The electric oven temperatures in this book are given for conventional ovens with top and bottom heat. When using a fan oven, the temperature should be decreased by about 20–40ºF / 10–20ºC – check the oven manufacturer's instruction book for further guidance. The cooking times given should be used as an approximate guideline only.

CONTENTS

ROAST CHICKEN WITH BORLOTTI BEANS AND TORTIGLIONI

Ingredients

1 small chicken, trussed

4 tbsp / 50 g butter, softened

1 bunch thyme

4 oz / 100 g tortiglioni or pasta tubes

4 cups / 1 liter chicken broth (stock)

4 large scallions (spring onions), peeled and green parts removed

½ small green cabbage, chopped

8 oz / 200 g sugar snap peas

2 cups / 400 g canned borlotti beans, drained and rinsed

8 sun-dried tomatoes, chopped

1 tbsp chopped parsley

Salt and freshly ground pepper

Method

Prep and cook time: 1 hour 35 min

1 Heat the oven to 425F (220C / Gas Mark 7).

2 Rub the chicken all over with the butter, place in an ovenproof dish and season with salt and pepper. Chop a few of the thyme leaves and scatter over the chicken. Put the remaining thyme in the cavity of the chicken.

3 Roast the chicken in the oven for about 1¼ hours, basting from time to time. Turn the oven down to 350 F (180 C / Gas Mark 4) after 20 minutes.

4 Half an hour before the end of cooking time, cook the pasta according to the package instructions. Drain well and rinse.

5 Bring the broth (stock) to a boil in a large pan and add the scallions (spring onions). Let boil for 5 minutes then add the cabbage and sugar snap peas.

6 Boil for 2 minutes then add the borlotti beans, cooked pasta, tomatoes and parsley. Heat through then pour the vegetables into the dish with the chicken. Return to the oven for 10 minutes and serve.

ROAST MONKFISH WITH TOMATOES AND OLIVES

Ingredients

4 tbsp olive oil

4 monkfish fillets, cut from
the tail end

1 lb / 450 g cherry tomatoes,
on the vine

1 garlic clove, chopped

1 red chili pepper, deseeded and
finely chopped

2 tbsp marjoram leaves

1 cup / 250 ml white wine

1 cup / 100 g black olives, very
finely chopped

Salt and freshly ground pepper

Method

Prep and cook time: 20 min

1 Heat the oven to 400F (200 C / Gas Mark 6).

2 Heat the oil in a large skillet and gently fry the monkfish for 2 minutes on each side.

3 Put the tomatoes in an ovenproof dish and lay the monkfish on top.

4 Fry the garlic and chili in the skillet until soft. Add the marjoram leaves and white wine and let bubble then pour over the monkfish and tomatoes. Season with salt and pepper.

5 Cover the dish with kitchen foil and cook in the oven for 8–10 minutes or until the fish is cooked through. Scatter over the olives and serve immediately.

DUCK WITH APPLE AND LENTILS

Ingredients

1 wild duck, oven-ready

Salt and freshly ground pepper

4 tbsp oil

6 shallots, sliced lengthways

2 stalks celery, chopped

2 large carrots, peeled and chopped

½ cup / 125 ml white wine

2 cups / 500 ml chicken broth (stock)

1 sprig parsley

4 tbsp / 50 g butter

1 small onion, finely chopped

1 cooking apple, peeled, cored and diced

1 cup / 200 g canned split lentils, drained and rinsed

Juice of ½ a lemon

Method

Prep and cook time: 1 hour 30 min

1 Heat the oven to 425F (220 C / Gas Mark 7).

2 Rub the duck with a little oil, salt and pepper and place in a deep ovenproof dish.

3 Heat the remaining oil in a large skillet and gently cook the shallots and celery until just softened. Stir in the carrots to coat them with oil then place the vegetables in the dish with the duck.

4 Pour the white wine and broth (stock) into the dish, place the parsley sprig on top of the bird and roast for 20 minutes.

5 Baste the duck with the cooking liquid, turn the heat down to 350F (180 C / Gas Mark 4) and roast for a further 45 minutes or until the duck is cooked through. Set aside and keep warm.

6 Melt the butter in a small pan and cook the onions for 5 minutes or until soft but not brown. Add the apple, lentils, lemon juice and about 2 tbsp of the duck cooking liquid. Season with salt and pepper and simmer for 6–8 minutes.

7 Serve the duck with the apple and lentil mixture alongside.

KLEFTIKO OF LAMB WITH FETA

Ingredients

1 small lamb shoulder,
about 3¼ lb / 1½ kg

6 tbsp olive oil

Salt and freshly ground pepper

4 shallots, sliced

6 garlic cloves, sliced

1 cup / 100 g black olives, sliced

2 tsp dried oregano

Juice of 1 lemon

2 bay leaves

8 oz / 200 g feta cheese, diced

Method

Prep and cook time: 4 hours

1 Heat the oven to 325F (160 C / Gas Mark 3).

2 Make small incisions in the skin of the lamb with a sharp knife. Rub a little of the oil all over the meat and sprinkle with salt.

3 Heat 3 tbsp of oil in a large skillet and sear the meat on both sides until lightly browned. Remove from the skillet and set aside.

4 Return the skillet to the heat and gently cook the shallots until just soft.

5 Lay 3 large sheets of kitchen parchment in a deep roasting pan, enough to make a parcel for the meat. Put the shallots in the middle of the parchment and lay the seared meat on top.

6 Insert the garlic and olive slices into the incisions in the meat and sprinkle over the oregano. Drizzle over the remaining oil and the lemon juice and lay the bay leaves on top.

7 Scatter any remaining garlic and olives around the meat, season with salt and pepper and fold the edges of the parchment together to make a loose parcel. Bake the parcel in the oven for 3 hours.

8 Remove the pan from the oven, open the top of the parcel and carefully baste the meat with the juices. Scatter the feta cheese around the meat, turn the heat up to 400 F (200C / Gas Mark 6) and return the pan to the oven for 20 minutes or until the meat is cooked through.

9 Let the meat rest in the pan for 15 minutes then transfer to a warmed serving dish and serve with the remaining contents of the parcel.

CHICKEN LEGS WITH APPLE

Ingredients

4 chicken legs

6 tbsp olive oil

2 tbsp honey

½ cup / 125 ml dry cider

12 shallots, peeled

4 dessert apples, cut into wedges and cored

Salt and freshly ground pepper

Sage leaves, to garnish

Method

Prep and cook time: 50 min

1 Heat the oven to 400 F (200C / Gas Mark 6).

2 Separate the chicken thighs from the drumsticks.

3 Heat the oil in a roasting pan and sear the chicken pieces until lightly browned on all sides. Remove from the pan and set aside.

4 Stir the honey and cider into the pan, let bubble then add the shallots. Stir for 2 minutes, season with salt and pepper then add the apples and coat them with the pan juices.

5 Return the chicken pieces to the pan, coat with the juices and cover with kitchen foil.

6 Roast in the oven for 30 minutes, or until the chicken is cooked through, basting frequently. Serve garnished with the sage leaves.

VEAL SHANK WITH RED WINE

Ingredients

4 tbsp olive oil

1 veal shank, about 3½ lb / 1½ kg

4 oz / 100 g pancetta, cubed

12 small shallots, peeled

2 carrots, chopped

6 tomatoes, deseeded and quartered

1 cup / 250 ml red wine

2 sprigs rosemary

1 garlic bulb, whole

Salt and freshly ground pepper

Method

Prep and cook time: 2 hours 20 min

1 Heat the oven to 350F (180C / Gas Mark 4).

2 Heat the oil in a flameproof dish and sear the veal shank until well browned on all sides. Remove from the pan and set aside.

3 Fry the pancetta in the dish until the fat begins to run then add the shallots and carrots. Stir for 2 minutes then add the tomatoes.

4 Return the meat to the dish, pour over the red wine and add the rosemary sprigs and garlic bulb. Season with salt and pepper, cover and place in the oven.

5 Cook for 2 hours, basting every 30 minutes, or until the meat is tender.

ROASTED SALMON WITH PEPPERS

Ingredients

4 pieces salmon fillet

Juice of 1 lemon

1 garlic clove

1 red bell pepper, deseeded
and cut into strips

1 yellow bell pepper, deseeded
and cut into strips

1 green bell pepper, deseeded
and cut into strips

1 onion, halved and sliced

7 tbsp / 100 ml vegetable or fish broth
(stock), or white wine

4 tbsp olive oil

1 tbsp fennel seeds

Salt and freshly ground pepper

Basil leaves, to garnish

Method

Prep and cook time: 50 min

1 Heat the oven to 400F (200C / Gas Mark 6).

2 Brush the fish with 2 tbsp lemon juice and leave
to stand for 10 minutes.

3 Halve the clove of garlic and rub the cut side over
the inside of an ovenproof dish.

4 Season the bell peppers and onion with salt and
pepper and place in the roasting dish. Pour over the
broth (stock) and drizzle with 2 tbsp oil.

5 Season the fish fillets with salt and pepper and
lay on top of the peppers. Sprinkle with the fennel
seeds, drizzle over the rest of the oil and lemon
juice and cover with foil.

6 Bake for 20–30 minutes or until the fish is cooked
through. Serve scattered with basil leaves.

TERIYAKI CHICKEN

Ingredients

3 tbsp honey

6 tbsp teriyaki sauce

2 tbsp vegetable oil

1 chicken, trussed

For the salad:

4 oz / 100 g snow peas (mangetout)

2 tbsp rice vinegar

1 tbsp lemon juice

3 tbsp sesame oil

½ tsp salt

2 carrots, peeled and finely
sliced lengthways

½ cucumber, peeled and finely
sliced lengthways

1 cup / 100 g soya bean sprouts

Method

Prep and cook time: 2 hours plus
2 hours to marinate

1 Mix the honey with the teriyaki sauce and oil
and brush the chicken with the mixture. Marinate for
2 hours.

2 Heat the oven to 400F (200C / Gas Mark 6). Place
the chicken on a rack in a roasting pan and roast for
20 minutes.

3 Turn the oven down to 350F (180C / Gas Mark 4),
baste the chicken with the marinade and roast for a
further 1 hour or until the chicken is cooked through,
basting every 20 minutes.

4 Remove the chicken from the oven and rest for
15 minutes.

5 Blanch the snow peas (mangetout) in boiling water
for 2 minutes. Drain, refresh in cold water and pat
dry with kitchen paper.

6 Mix together the rice vinegar, lemon juice, sesame
oil and salt and toss into the salad vegetables and
snow peas.

7 Serve the chicken with the salad.

ROASTED WINTER SQUASH AND FENNEL

Ingredients

4 tbsp olive oil

1 medium squash, peeled, deseeded and diced

2 bulbs fennel

1 cup / 175 g chopped dates

Salt and freshly ground pepper

Method

Prep and cook time: 35 min

1 Heat the oven to 350F (180C / Gas Mark 4).

2 Heat the oil in a large skillet and gently fry the squash for 2 minutes.

3 Chop the green tops of the fennel and set aside. Chop the fennel flesh and add to the squash. Stir well and transfer to a roasting pan. Pour over 1 cup / 250 ml water and roast in the oven for 15 minutes.

4 Stir the fennel tops and dates into the vegetables, season with salt and pepper and return to the oven for 10 minutes or until the vegetables are golden brown.

CHICKEN LEGS WITH EGGPLANT AND LEMON

Ingredients

8 tbsp olive oil

1 tsp ground cumin

1 tsp paprika

1 tsp salt

Juice of 1 lemon

4 chicken legs

1 red onion, sliced

2 medium eggplants (aubergines), sliced

2 lemons, washed and sliced

Salt and freshly ground pepper

Cilantro (fresh coriander), to garnish

Method

Prep and cook time: 50 min

1 Heat the oven to 350F (180C / Gas Mark4).

2 Mix 2 tbsp of the oil with the cumin, paprika, salt and lemon juice.

3 Separate the chicken thighs from the drumsticks, rub each piece with the cumin mixture and set aside.

4 Rub the sliced onions with a little oil and set aside.

5 Heat 2 tbsp oil in a ridged grill pan and grill the eggplant (aubergine) slices in batches for 1 minute on each side. Set aside and keep warm.

6 Heat the grill pan until smoking and sear the chicken pieces on all sides until lightly browned.

7 Put the chicken pieces in an ovenproof dish, tuck the eggplant, onion and lemon slices all around and drizzle with the remaining oil and the scrapings from the grill pan.

8 Season with salt and pepper and roast for 30 minutes, or until the chicken is cooked through, basting once. Serve garnished with cilantro (coriander) leaves.

CHICKEN LEGS WITH POTATOES AND SWEETCORN

Ingredients

4 chicken legs

1 tbsp honey

1 tsp sambal oelek or chili paste

1 tsp wine vinegar

2 lb / 900 g potatoes, peeled and cut into wedges

4 shallots, peeled and cut into wedges

4 tbsp vegetable oil

2 sprigs rosemary

1 cup / 200 g canned corn, drained and rinsed

Salt and freshly ground pepper

Method

Prep and cook time: 1 hour

1 Heat the oven to 350F (180 C / Gas Mark 4).

2 Mix together the honey, sambal oelek and vinegar and season with salt and pepper. Rub the mixture into the chicken legs.

3 Put the potatoes and shallots in a roasting pan and drizzle with the oil. Lay the chicken legs on top and scatter over the rosemary.

4 Roast in the oven for 20 minutes then baste the chicken with the juices and stir in the corn.

5 Return to the oven and cook for a further 20 minutes or until the juices from the meat run clear.

LEG OF LAMB
STUDDED WITH GARLIC
AND ROSEMARY

Ingredients

1 leg of lamb, about 3 lb / 1.2 kg

4 tbsp olive oil

4 sprigs rosemary

8 garlic cloves, peeled and thickly sliced

2 tbsp Dijon mustard

2 tbsp clear honey

Rosemary sprigs, to garnish

Salt and freshly ground pepper

Method

Prep and cook time: 1 hour 10 min

1 Heat the oven to 400F (200 C / Gas Mark 6.)

2 Rub the lamb all over with the oil and sprinkle with salt and pepper.

3 Using a sharp knife cut short incisions ¾ inch / 2 cm deep all over the skin of the meat and insert a sprig of rosemary or slices of garlic into each one.

4 Put the meat in a roasting pan, pour in 1 cup (250 ml) water and roast in the oven for 20 minutes. Baste the meat and turn the oven down to 375F (190 C / Gas Mark 5).

5 Roast for another 20 minutes, then mix together the mustard and honey and brush it over the meat.

6 Return to the oven for 20 minutes or until the meat juices run clear. Let the meat rest for 15 minutes before serving. Serve garnished with rosemary.

ROAST BEEF AND YORKSHIRE PUDDING

Ingredients

For the Yorkshire puddings:

1 egg

½ cup / 125 ml milk

2 tbsp water

⅔ cup / 75 g all-purpose (plain) flour

Salt and pepper

2 tbsp vegetable oil

For the beef:

1 piece beef fillet, about 2.2 lb / 1 kg

½ cup / 125 ml vegetable oil

1 tbsp chopped rosemary

1 tbsp chopped thyme

Method

Prep and cook time: 1 hour 40 min

1 Heat the oven to 425F (220C / Gas Mark 7).

2 First, make the Yorkshire pudding batter. Beat the egg, milk and water into the flour to make a smooth batter, season with salt and pepper and set aside.

3 For the beef, rub a little oil over the meat and season with salt and pepper. Heat 7 tbsp / 100 ml of the oil in a roasting pan and sear the meat until browned all over.

4 Mix the remaining oil with the rosemary and thyme and spread over the top of the meat. Put to roast in the oven.

5 After 10 minutes move the meat down to the middle or bottom shelf and turn the heat down to 400F (200C / Gas Mark 6).

6 After the meat has been cooking for 45 minutes in total, check to see if it is cooked to your liking. Remove from the roasting pan and keep warm.

7 To finish the Yorkshire puddings, grease patty pans with the oil and place on the top shelf in the oven for 5 minutes. Pour the batter into the patty pans and return to the oven for about 15 minutes or until the puddings are risen and golden brown. Serve the beef and Yorkshire puddings with roasted parsnips and potatoes.

ROSEMARY CHICKEN ON ROAST VEGETABLES

Ingredients

4 tbsp / 50 g butter, softened

1 medium chicken

2 tbsp chopped rosemary leaves

1 lemon, halved

3 tbsp vegetable oil

2 large carrots, peeled and sliced lengthways

4 small parsnips, peeled and sliced lengthways

6 new potatoes, scrubbed and sliced lengthways

12 garlic cloves, in their skins

Salt and freshly ground pepper

Rosemary sprigs, to garnish

Method

Prep and cook time: 1 hour 40 min

1 Heat the oven to 400F (200C / Gas Mark 6).

2 Rub the butter all over the chicken and sprinkle with salt and pepper. Scatter over half the rosemary leaves and put the remainder in the cavity along with the lemon halves.

3 Heat the oil in a roasting pan over a medium heat and add the vegetables, stirring so they are coated with the oil.

4 Place the chicken in the middle of the pan and roast in the oven for 20 minutes. Baste the meat, turn the vegetables and turn the heat down to 350F (190C / Gas Mark 5).

5 Roast for a further 30 minutes then baste again and add the garlic to the pan. Return to the oven and cook for another 30 minutes or until the meat juices run clear.

6 Serve garnished with rosemary sprigs.

MOROCCAN ROAST LAMB

Ingredients

1 shoulder of lamb,
about 4½ lb / 2 kg

2 tbsp vegetable oil

1 tbsp harissa

1 tbsp honey

1 tbsp fennel seeds

1 tbsp cumin seeds

1 tbsp coriander seeds

1 tbsp chopped rosemary leaves

2 cups / 500 ml lamb broth
(stock), hot

1 lb / 450 g pumpkin or squash,
peeled and cut into chunks

8 oz / 200 g dates

Salt and freshly ground pepper

Method

Prep and cook time: 1 hour 40 min plus
2 hours to marinate

1 Score the skin of the lamb in a crisscross pattern.
Mix the oil, harissa and honey and season with salt
and pepper. Stir in the spices and rosemary leaves
and rub the mixture into the meat. Set aside to
marinate for 2 hours.

2 Heat the oven to 375F (190 C / Gas Mark 5). Put
the meat in a roasting pan, cover with kitchen foil
and roast in the oven for 45 minutes, basting every
15 minutes.

3 Remove the foil, pour in the hot lamb broth
(stock) and add the pumpkin and dates. Turn the
oven up to 400 F (200C / Gas Mark 6) and roast
for a further 40 minutes or until the meat is cooked
through and the pumpkin is tender.

4 Rest the meat in a warm place for 15 minutes
before serving.

ROAST PORK WITH CRACKLING, GARLIC AND LEMON

Ingredients

1 piece pork loin, about 2.2 lb / 1 kg boned and rolled

1 tbsp salt

3 tbsp olive oil

1 onion, cut into wedges

2 parsnips, peeled and cut lengthways

1 celery stalk, cut lengthways

2 carrots, peeled and cut lengthways

1 lemon, scrubbed and cut into wedges

6 garlic cloves, skin on

1 tbsp balsamic vinegar

Method

Prep and cook time: 1 hour 30 min

1 Heat the oven to 425F (220C / Gas Mark 7).

2 Score the fat on the pork with a sharp knife and pour over a kettle of boiling water. Pat dry thoroughly with kitchen paper and rub the salt all over the meat.

3 Heat the oil in a roasting pan and sear the two short ends of the pork. Place skin side up and roast in the oven for 30 minutes.

4 Turn the oven down to 350 F (180 C / Gas Mark 4) and add the prepared vegetables, lemon and garlic to the roasting pan. Baste with the meat juices and return the pan to the oven for a further 40–50 minutes, basting from time to time.

5 Remove the meat from the pan when it is cooked through and set aside in a warm place to rest for 15 minutes.

6 Put the pan on the heat and deglaze the juices with the balsamic vinegar. Serve the meat juices drizzled over the meat and roast vegetables.

DUCK WITH ORANGE

Ingredients

1 oven-ready duck, about
3½ lb / 1½ kg

4 oranges, scrubbed and cut into
wedges

2 sprigs thyme

4 tbsp red wine

Scant 1 cup / 200 ml chicken
broth (stock)

Salt and freshly ground pepper

Method

Prep and cook time: 1 hour 50 min

1 Heat the oven to 425F (220 C / Gas Mark 7).

2 Prick the duck skin all over with a sharp needle to allow the fat to run out. Remove any large clumps of fat from the cavity of the duck and rub the cavity and skin with salt and pepper.

3 Put the wedges from 1 orange into the cavity with the thyme sprigs and put the duck in a roasting pan.

4 Roast in the oven for 20 minutes then carefully drain off the excess fat. Turn the oven down to 350 F (180C / Gas Mark 4) and roast for another 30 minutes.

5 Drain off the fat once again, but retain the meat juices. Baste the duck and tuck the remaining orange wedges around it. Return to the oven for another 30–40 minutes or until the juices from the thickest part of the duck legs run clear.

6 Remove the duck and orange wedges from the pan and keep warm.

7 To make the gravy, drain off the fat from the meat juices and heat the juices. Add the the wine to the meat juices, let bubble then add the broth (stock). Simmer for 5 minutes and season with salt and pepper.

ROAST TURKEY

Ingredients

1 oven-ready turkey, about
5½ lb / 2½ kg

2 tsp of each: salt, pepper, sweet
paprika

2 cooking apples, peeled, cored
and diced

Juice of 1 lemon

1½ cup / 200 g hazelnuts, chopped

²/₃ cup / 100 g ground almonds

2 tsp ground cinnamon

6 tbsp / 75 g butter

Salt and freshly ground pepper

For the sausage rolls:

6 slices bacon

12 cocktail sausages

2 tbsp / 25 g butter

For the gravy:

½ cup / 125 ml white wine

1¼ cups / 300 ml chicken broth
(stock)

Scant 1 cup / 200 ml cream

Method

Prep and cook time: 3 hours 30 min

1 Heat the oven to 400F (200 C / Gas Mark 6).

2 Rub the salt, pepper and paprika into the cavity of
the turkey.

3 Mix together the diced apples and the lemon juice
then stir in the hazelnuts, almonds and cinnamon.
Stuff the mixture into the cavity of the turkey and sew
the opening together with strong thread.

4. Rub the outside of the turkey with the butter,
season with salt and pepper and place in a deep
roasting pan.

5 Roast the turkey in the oven for 1 hour then
baste with the juices and return to the oven for about
1½ hours, basting every 30 minutes. When the
juices from the thickest part of the turkey legs run
clear remove the turkey from the pan, set aside and
keep warm. It should rest for at least 20 minutes
before serving.

6 For the bacon sausages, cut each bacon rasher in
half, wrap each piece around a sausage and secure
with a toothpick (cocktail stick). Melt the butter in
a skillet and fry the bacon-wrapped sausages on all
sides until cooked through. Set aside and keep warm.

7 To make the gravy, heat the juices in the roasting
pan. Add the wine and the chicken broth (stock),
boil for 5 minutes then stir in the cream. Let bubble,
season with salt and pepper and serve hot with the
turkey and sausages.

PORK FILLET WITH BAKED PLUMS

Ingredients

1½ lb / 650 g pork fillet

6 tbsp olive oil

4 large potatoes, peeled

1 celery stalk, finely chopped

1 garlic clove, crushed

Zest of 1 lemon

1 egg, beaten

1 tbsp chopped parsley

1 tbsp chopped thyme

6 slices streaky bacon

2 tbsp wholegrain mustard

1 onion, cut into wedges

6 red plums, stones removed and cut into wedges

Salt and freshly ground pepper

Method

Prep and cook time: 1 hour 20 min

1 Heat the oven to 375F (190C / Gas Mark 5).

2 Lay the pork fillet skin side down and brush the flesh with about 2 tbsp oil.

3 Boil 2 of the potatoes, mash them and add the celery, garlic, lemon zest, egg, parsley and thyme. Season with salt and pepper, spread onto the pork and roll the fillet up tightly.

4 Lay the bacon slices over the meat, secure with kitchen twine and spread the mustard on top of the meat.

5 Heat the remaining oil in a roasting pan. Cut the remaining potatoes into wedges and coat with the oil in the pan. Put the meat into the pan and then roast in the oven for 30 minutes.

6 Add the onion wedges to the pan, baste the meat, potatoes and onions, and return the pan to the oven for 20 minutes.

7 Add the plum wedges and roast for a further 10 minutes. Let the meat rest for 15 minutes before serving.

SPARE RIBS

Ingredients

2 tbsp soft brown sugar

1 tbsp soy sauce

2 tsp mustard powder

2 garlic cloves, crushed

2 tbsp tomato ketchup

1 tbsp Worcestershire sauce

2 tbsp red wine vinegar

1 tsp salt

1 tsp black pepper

3½ lb / 1½ kg spare ribs

Method

Prep and cook time: 1 hour plus
2 hours to marinate

1 Mix together the all the ingredients except the ribs to make a marinade. Coat the ribs and leave to marinate for at least 2 hours, turning from time to time.

2 Heat the oven to 350F (180C / Gas Mark 4).

3 Place the ribs in a roasting pan, pour over the marinade so they are all well coated and roast for about 45 minutes, basting frequently, until the ribs are tender.

SHOULDER OF LAMB WITH TOMATOES, OLIVES AND PINE NUTS

Ingredients

1 lamb shoulder, trimmed

4 tbsp olive oil

1 sprig rosemary

1 sprig sage

1 bay leaf

1 onion, finely chopped

2 garlic cloves, finely chopped

3 tbsp pine nuts

3½ cups / 800 ml lamb broth (stock)

10 oz / 250 g cherry tomatoes

2 cups / 200 g black olives

Salt and freshly ground pepper

Method

Prep and cook time: 1 hour 45 min

1 Heat the oven to 350F (180C / Gas Mark 4).

2 Rub the lamb shoulder all over with salt and pepper. Heat the oil in a large skillet and sear the meat on all sides. Transfer the meat to a roasting pan, tuck the rosemary, sage and bay leaf under the meat and cover with kitchen foil. Roast in the oven for 1–1½ hours or until the meat juices run clear, basting every 30 minutes.

3 Meanwhile, reheat the oil in the skillet and gently fry the chopped onion until translucent. Add the garlic, stir for 1 minutes then add the pine nuts. Swirl the pan around until the pine nuts start to brown then pour over a scant 1 cup (200 ml) lamb broth (stock). Let simmer for 5 minutes then set aside.

4 When the meat is cooked, remove from the roasting pan and keep warm. Put the tomatoes into the roasting pan, discarding the herbs, and cook for 10 minutes. Reheat the onion and pine nut mixture, season with salt and pepper and pour over the meat. Serve with the tomatoes and the olives scattered over.

Tip: Use the remaining lamb broth to make a gravy. When you have removed the tomatoes from the roasting pan, heat the meat juices and pour in the remaining broth. Bring to a boil, stirring all the time, and season with salt and pepper.

ROAST BEEF WITH PECORINO AND POLENTA

Ingredients

1 cup / 150 g cornmeal (polenta)

¾ cup / 100 g pecorino, grated

4 tbsp / 50 g butter

1 egg, beaten

Salt and freshly ground pepper

5 tbsp olive oil

2 lb / 900 g beef fillet, trimmed of fat

2 tsp chopped thyme

2 tsp chopped sage

2 tsp chopped rosemary

1 sprig thyme

1 sprig rosemary sprigs

12 sage leaves

Method

Prep and cook time: 1 h 10 min

1 Heat the oven to 200C (400F / Gas Mark 6).

2 Cook the cornmeal (polenta) according to packet instructions then beat in the pecorino, butter and egg until you have a thick paste – add a little more water if necessary. Season with salt and pepper and keep warm.

3 Heat 3 tbsp oil in a roasting pan and sear the meat all over until well browned. Sprinkle with salt, pepper and half the chopped herbs then spread the polenta over the top and sides of the meat. Set the remaining polenta aside and keep warm.

4 Spread the remaining oil and chopped herbs over the meat, tuck the other herbs around and roast in the oven for 25 minutes (rare), 35 minutes (medium) or 45 minutes (well done).

5 Let rest for 10 minutes and serve with the remaining cornmeal alongside.

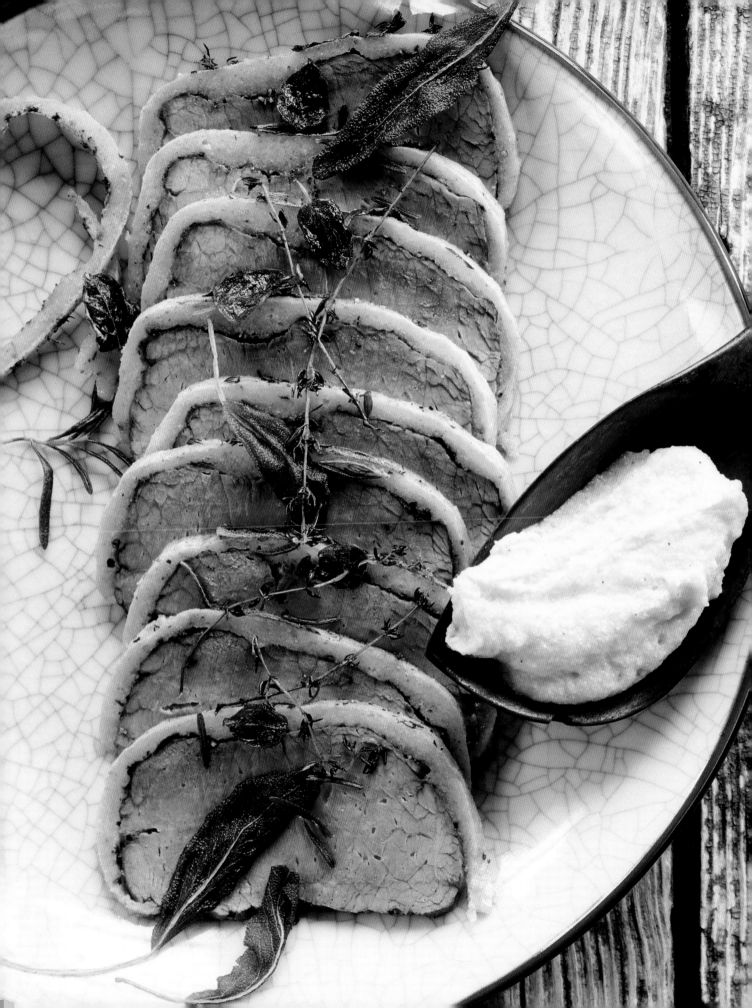

CHICKEN WITH BACON AND ROOT VEGETABLES

Ingredients

2 carrots, peeled and cut into chunks

1 small celery root (celeriac), peeled and cut into chunks

4 medium potatoes, peeled and cut into chunks

2 parsnips, peeled and cut into chunks

1 cup / 250 ml white wine

1 cup / 250 ml chicken broth (stock)

1 sprig thyme, chopped

1 sprig rosemary, chopped

3 garlic cloves, chopped

1 chicken, trussed

2 tbsp olive oil

3 slices bacon

Salt and freshly ground pepper

Method

Prep and cook time: 1 hour 45 min

1 Heat the oven to 400F (200C / Gas Mark 6).

2 Put the vegetables into a large roasting pan, pour over the wine and broth (stock) and scatter over the herbs and garlic.

3 Rub the chicken with the oil, season with salt and pepper and place on top of the vegetables. Lay the bacon slices over the chicken and cover with kitchen foil.

4 Roast in the oven for 1 hour, basting the chicken and turning the vegetables every 20 minutes.

5 Remove the foil and roast for a further 20 minutes or until the chicken is golden brown and cooked through. The chicken is cooked when a skewer is inserted into the thickest part of the thigh and the juices run clear.

6 Let the chicken rest for 15 minutes before serving.

ROAST BEEF
WITH HONEY SAUCE

Ingredients

3 tbsp olive oil

1 tbsp wholegrain mustard

2 tsp honey

Salt and freshly ground pepper

2 lb / 900 g beef fillet, with fat

1⅓ cups / 300 ml beef broth (stock)

Method

Prep and cook time: 1 h 10 min

1 Heat the oven to 240C (450F / Gas Mark 8).

2 Mix together 2 tbsp oil, the mustard and honey, season with salt and pepper and rub into the meat.

3 Heat the remaining oil in a roasting pan and sear the meat on all sides until browned then roast in the oven for 20 minutes (rare), 25 minutes (medium) or 35 minutes (well done).

4 Pour the beef broth (stock) into the pan, baste the meat and return to the oven for 15 minutes. Remove the meat from the pan and rest in a warm place for 15 minutes before serving.

5 While the meat is resting, put the roasting pan on the heat, let the juices bubble stirring all the time, and serve with the meat and vegetables of your choice.

ROAST PARTRIDGE WITH PEARS AND POMEGRANATE SEEDS

Ingredients

4 oven-ready partridges

4 tbsp olive oil

Salt and freshly ground pepper

1$\frac{1}{3}$ cups / 300 ml white wine

$\frac{2}{3}$ cup / 150 ml honey

2 onions, peeled and sliced into thick slices

4 pears, peeled

2 cups / 150 g pomegranate seeds

Method

Prep and cook time: 1 h

1 Heat the oven to 200C (400F / Gas Mark 6).

2 Rub the partridges inside and out with the oil, season with salt and pepper and place in roasting pan. Roast in the oven for 20 minutes.

3 Heat the wine and honey in a small pan. Remove the partridges from the oven and add the wine/honey mixture to the pan.

4 Add the onions and pears, baste them and the partridges with the pan juices and return to the oven for 20 minutes, basting once more during cooking.

5 Let the partridges rest for 10 minutes then serve with the pomegranate seeds sprinkled over.

SEA BREAM
WITH HERB CRUST

Ingredients

2 sea bream, each about 1lb / 450 g, cleaned and gutted

4 tbsp olive oil

2 garlic cloves

2 cups / 100 g fresh breadcrumbs

3 tbsp chopped parsley

2 tbsp chopped thyme

Juice of 1 lemon

2 lemons, sliced

Salt and freshly ground pepper

Method
Prep and cook time: 35 min

1 Heat the oven to 450F (230C / Gas Mark 8).

2 Cut 3 slashes along each side of the fish with a sharp knife. Rub the fish all over with a little oil and place each fish on a large sheet of kitchen parchment.

3 Heat the remaining oil in a skillet and gently cook the garlic until soft. Stir in the breadcrumbs, parsley, thyme and lemon juice and season with salt and pepper.

4 Tuck the lemon slices into the slashes, the belly and the mouth of the fish. Scatter the herb crust over the fish and scrunch the edges of the parchment together to make a parcel.

5 Bake in the oven for 25 minutes and serve immediately.

ROAST CHICKEN
WITH LEMON

Ingredients

4 tbsp olive oil

4 chicken legs, thighs separated from drumsticks

12 garlic cloves, skins on

2 red chilies, deseeded and finely chopped

2 lemons, washed and sliced

4 sprigs thyme

½ cup / 125 ml chicken broth (stock)

Salt and freshly ground pepper

Method

Prep and cook time: 50 min

1 Heat the oven to 350F (180C / Gas Mark 4).

2 Heat the oil in a roasting pan and brown the chicken pieces on all sides.

3 Add the garlic and chopped chilies to the pan, coat with oil then tuck lemon slices in between the chicken pieces.

4 Strip the leaves from the thyme sprigs and scatter over the chicken. Season with salt and pepper and pour over the broth (stock).

5 Cover with kitchen foil and roast in the oven for 30–40 minutes or until the chicken is cooked through, basting from time to time.

ROAST BEEF
WITH MUSHROOMS AND BACON

Ingredients

1 whole beef fillet, about 3¾ lb / 1.75 kg

6 tbsp olive oil

Salt and freshly ground pepper

4 slices bacon, chopped into pieces

1 leek, trimmed and finely chopped

2 carrots, peeled and finely chopped

10 oz / 300 g button mushrooms

7 tbsp / 100 ml marsala wine

Method

Prep and cook time: 1 h 15 min

1 Heat the oven to 425F (220C / Gas Mark 7).

2 Rub the meat with a little oil and season with salt and pepper.

3 Heat the remaining oil in a roasting pan and fry the bacon for 3 minutes. Remove from the pan and set aside.

4 Sear the meat on all sides in the pan and set aside.

5 Put the chopped leek and carrot into the pan, stir until the leek starts to soften then add the mushrooms and stir in the marsala wine.

6 Return the meat and bacon to the pan, baste in the pan juices, cover with kitchen foil and roast in the oven for 25 minutes (rare), 35 minutes (medium) or 45 minutes (well done).

7 Let the meat rest for at least 15 minutes before serving.

ROASTED PORK RIBS WITH CABBAGE

Ingredients

For the pork ribs:

4 tbsp vegetable oil

1 garlic clove, crushed

2 tbsp honey

1 tbsp English mustard

Juice of 1 lemon

Salt and freshly ground pepper

3½ lb / 1.5 kg ribs

Oil, for roasting

For the cabbage:

2 tbsp oil

1 onion, finely chopped

1 white cabbage, shredded

1 cup / 250 ml vegetable broth (stock) or water

2 tbsp cumin seeds

1 tbsp butter

1 handful spinach, shredded

Salt and freshly ground pepper

Thyme leaves, to garnish

Method

Prep and cook time: 2 h plus 2 h to marinate

1 For the ribs, mix together the vegetable oil, garlic, honey, mustard and lemon juice. Season with salt and pepper and rub into the ribs. Leave to marinade for at least 2 hours.

2 Heat the oven to 350F (180C / Gas Mark 4).

3 Put the ribs in a roasting pan, drizzle over a little oil and roast in the oven for about 45 minutes, basting from time to time, until the ribs are cooked and tender.

4 Meanwhile, cook the cabbage. Heat the oil in a pan and cook the onion until softened but not brown. Add the cabbage and stir well to coat with the oil.

5 Pour over the broth (stock) and simmer until the cabbage is just tender, stirring from time to time. Drain then stir in the cumin seeds, butter and spinach and season with salt and pepper. Serve the ribs and cabbage garnished with thyme leaves.

VENISON WITH CREAMED CABBAGE

Ingredients

for 6 servings

2 lb 8 oz / 1.2 kg venison haunch, boned and rolled

4 tbsp / 50 g butter

1 tbsp black peppercorns, lightly crushed

1 tbsp juniper berries, lightly crushed

12 slices bacon

1 onion, peeled and roughly chopped

1 carrot, peeled and roughly chopped

1 small celeriac, peeled and roughly chopped

1 leek, sliced

½ cup / 125 ml red wine

2 cups / 500 ml game broth (stock)

Pinch sugar

For the creamed cabbage:

1 medium Savoy cabbage, shredded

2 tbsp / 25 g butter

1 onion, finely sliced

4 slices bacon, finely chopped

7 tbsp / 100 ml chicken broth

7/8 cup / 200 ml whipping cream

Pinch ground nutmeg

Method

Prep and cook time: 2 h 30 min

1 Heat the oven to 350F (180 C / Gas Mark 4).

2 Season the venison with salt and pepper. Heat 2 tablespoons of the butter in a large skillet and brown the meat on all sides. Remove the meat from the pan and press the crushed peppercorns and juniper berries into the surface. Wrap the meat in the bacon slices and secure with kitchen twine.

3 Heat the remaining butter in a large ovenproof dish and gently cook the vegetables until soft but not brown. Add the meat then pour over the red wine, let it bubble then add the broth and sugar. Season with salt and pepper then cover the dish and place in the oven for 1½–2 hours or until the venison is tender.

4 When the venison is cooked, remove the dish from the oven and set it aside to rest for 15–20 minutes.

5 For the creamed cabbage, cook the chopped cabbage in boiling, salted water for 3 minutes then drain well and refresh under cold water.

6 Heat the butter in a large pan, gently cook the onion for 2 minutes then add the chopped bacon and cook until the bacon is browned.

7 Add the drained cabbage, pour in the broth and cream and cook gently for 5–6 minutes, stirring from time to time. Season with salt, pepper and the nutmeg and serve alongside the venison.

BALSAMIC APPLES AND RED ONIONS

Ingredients

4 tbsp olive oil

2 red onions, cut into wedges

2 large cooking apples, peeled, cored and cut into quarters

Salt and freshly ground pepper

2 tbsp balsamic vinegar

Method

Prep and cook time: 35 min

1 Heat the oven to 400F (200C / Gas Mark 6).

2 Heat the oil in a roasting pan and add the onions. Cook for 2 minutes then add the apples and stir so everything is coated with oil.

3 Season with salt and pepper, cover with kitchen foil and roast in the oven for 10 minutes.

4 Remove from the oven and discard the foil. Sprinkle the balsamic vinegar over the onions and apples, baste well and return to the oven for 10 more minutes.

ROAST HAM WITH PISTACHIOS

Ingredients

1 boned ham joint, about 2.2 lb / 1 kg, with skin

1 onion, roughly chopped

1 carrot, roughly chopped

2 bay leaves

3 tbsp vegetable oil

4 tbsp honey

2 tsp paprika

Salt and freshly ground pepper

2 cups / 500 g pistachio nuts

Fresh herbs, to garnish

Method

Prep and cook time:1 h 40 min

1 Put the ham joint in a large pan of water and bring to a boil. Pour the water away, refill the pan with fresh water and put in the onion, carrot and bay leaves. Bring to a boil and simmer for 40 minutes.

2 Heat the oven to 400F (200 C / Gas Mark 6).

3 Remove the cooked ham from the pan, cut away and discard the skin and fat and pat the meat dry with kitchen paper.

4 Heat the oil with the honey and paprika in a small pan, season with salt and pepper and brush all over the meat.

5 Chop half the pistachios very finely until they resemble breadcrumbs. Chop the other half very coarsely.

6 Brush the ham with the oil and honey mixture once more then sprinkle the finely chopped pistachios over, pressing so they stick to the meat.

7 Put the meat in a roasting pan, sprinkle over the coarsely chopped pistachios and roast in the oven for 20 minutes. Serve garnished with fresh herbs.

LEG OF LAMB WITH EGGPLANT AND TZATZIKI

Ingredients

1 boned leg of lamb,
about 3 lb / 1.2 kg

About ½ cup / 125 ml olive oil

1 medium eggplant (aubergine),
cut into chunks

1 onion, chopped

3 garlic cloves, chopped

2 tsp ground cinnamon

2 tbsp honey

4 tbsp red wine vinegar

Salt and freshly ground pepper

2 tsp dried oregano

For the tzatziki:

½ cucumber, peeled, deseeded
and grated

2 garlic cloves, crushed

1 cup / 250 ml yogurt

1 tbsp olive oil

Juice of ½ lemon

12 mint leaves, shredded

Salt and freshly ground pepper

Mint leaves, to garnish

Method

Prep and cook time: 2 h

1 Lay the lamb flesh side up on a board and rub with a little oil.

2 Heat 4 tbsp oil in a large skillet and gently cook the eggplant (aubergine) until lightly browned – add more oil if needed. Remove the eggplant from the skillet and set aside.

3 Add 2 tbsp oil to the pan and cook the onion until soft then stir in the garlic and cinnamon. Cook for 2 minutes then add the honey and vinegar and season with salt and pepper. Let bubble then stir in the eggplant.

4 Heat the oven to 400F (200 C / Gas Mark 6).

5 Spread the eggplant mixture onto the lamb and roll tightly, securing with kitchen twine. Put the lamb into a roasting pan, brush with the remaining oil and sprinkle over the oregano, salt and pepper.

6 Roast in the oven for 20 minutes then turn the heat down to 325F (170C / Gas Mark 3). Baste the meat and roast for a further 1¼ hours, basting frequently. Rest the meat in a warm place for 15 minutes before serving.

7 While the meat is cooking, make the tzatziki. Put the grated cucumber in a colander, sprinkle with salt and set aside for 30 minutes. Mix the garlic into the yogurt with the oil and lemon juice and season with salt and pepper. Squeeze the excess moisture from the cucumber, mix into the yogurt and add the shredded mint leaves. Serve alongside the meat.

RACK OF LAMB
WITH AN ALMOND CRUST AND PEARS

Ingredients

3 tbsp olive oil

1 small onion, finely chopped

2 garlic cloves, finely chopped

½ cup / 25 g fresh breadcrumbs

1 tbsp chopped rosemary

1 tbsp chopped parsley

2 cups / 150 g chopped almonds

Salt and freshly ground pepper

1 egg, beaten

2 tbsp honey

2 racks lamb, French trimmed

Oil

1 onion, cut into wedges

2 pears, cut into wedges

1 bunch arugula (rocket)

1 sprig rosemary, to garnish

Method

Prep and cook time: 50 min

1 Heat the oven to 400F (200 C / Gas Mark 6).

2 Heat the oil in a skillet and gently fry the onion until soft. Add the garlic, cook for 2 minutes then stir in the breadcrumbs, rosemary, parsley and chopped almonds.

3 Season with salt and pepper then mix in the beaten egg.

4 Smear the honey over the fat of the lamb racks, press the almond mixture onto them and place in a roasting pan.

5 Rub the onion wedges with a little oil and tuck around the lamb racks. Roast for 15 minutes then add the pear wedges and roast for 10 more minutes.

6 Serve with arugula (rocket) and garnish with the rosemary sprig.

ROASTED VEGETABLES WITH APPLES

Ingredients

6 tbsp olive oil

4 small red onions, outer skins removed

4 medium new potatoes, scrubbed and cut into wedges

4 sprigs thyme

Salt and freshly ground pepper

4 small dessert apples

12 oz / 300 g cherry tomatoes, on the vine

1 tbsp balsamic vinegar

Method

Prep and cook time: 50 min

1 Heat the oven to 350F (180 C / Gas Mark 4).

2 Heat the oil in a roasting pan and add the onions and potatoes, coat with the hot oil and add the thyme sprigs. Sprinkle with salt and pepper and put into the oven to roast for 20 minutes.

3 Add the apples and tomatoes to the pan, baste everything with the cooking juices and return to the oven for 20 minutes.

4 Drizzle over the balsamic vinegar, transfer to a warmed serving dish and serve immediately.

GOOSE LEGS WITH PRUNES

Ingredients

4 goose legs

Salt

2 tbsp vegetable oil

1 onion, chopped

2 large carrots, peeled and diced

3 garlic cloves, chopped

8 oz / 200 g celery root (celeriac), peeled and diced

1 small cooking apple, peeled, cored and diced

3 tbsp cognac

½ cup / 125 ml red wine

½ cup / 125 ml chicken broth (stock)

Freshly ground pepper

1 sprig bay leaves

1½ cups / 250 g prunes

Method

Prep and cook time: 1 h 20 min

1 Heat the oven to 350F (180C / Gas Mark 4).

2 Rub the goose legs all over with salt.

3 Heat the oil in a large skillet and sear the goose legs until browned all over. Remove the legs from the skillet and place in an ovenproof dish.

4 Gently cook the onion in the skillet until softened then add the carrots, garlic, celery root (celeriac) and apple and stir for 2 minutes.

5 Pour over the cognac, red wine and chicken broth (stock) and let bubble then season with pepper. Pour the mixture into the dish around the goose legs, lay the sprig of bay leaves on top and roast in the oven for 20 minutes.

6 Pour away some of the fat in the dish, baste the goose legs with the remaining liquid and turn the oven down to 320 F (160 C / Gas Mark 3). Add the prunes and roast for a further 40 minutes, or until the juices from the goose legs run clear, basting once.

7 Pour away any excess fat, check the seasoning and serve immediately.

ROAST LAMB
WITH VEGETABLES

Ingredients

1 leg of lamb, about 4½ lb / 2kg

4 tbsp olive oil

Salt and freshly ground pepper

1 onion, finely chopped

4 garlic cloves, chopped

1 tsp fennel seeds

3 tbsp rosemary leaves, chopped

²/₃ cup / 75 g pine nuts, finely chopped

8 small potatoes, scrubbed and sliced

4 tomatoes, halved

1 cup / 100 g black olives

1 cup / 100 g green olives

1 red onion, finely sliced

1 handful arugula (rocket)

Method

Prep and cook time: 1 h 45 min

1 Heat the oven to 350F (180C / Gas Mark 4).

2 Score the skin of the lamb with a sharp knife and rub the meat all over with a little oil, salt and pepper. Place in a deep roasting pan.

3 Heat the remaining oil in a skillet and gently fry the onion until soft. Add the garlic, fennel seeds, rosemary and pine nuts and remove from the heat.

4 Cover the top of the lamb with the onion mixture, pressing it firmly into the flesh. Roast for 1 hour, basting every 20 minutes.

5 Put the sliced potatoes around the meat and return to the oven for 20 minutes or until the meat is cooked through.

6 Remove the meat from the pan and keep warm. Turn the oven up to 400 F (200C / Gas Mark 6) and put the tomatoes in alongside the potatoes. Roast for 15 minutes then remove from the oven and add the olives.

7 Serve the meat with the roast vegetables alongside and the red onion and arugula (rocket) scattered over.

ROLLED PORK ROAST WITH HERBS AND PINE NUTS

Ingredients

3 tbsp olive oil plus extra for rubbing

1 onion, chopped

3 garlic cloves, chopped

2 red chilies, deseeded and finely chopped

1½ cups / 150 g pine nuts

1 cup / 50 g fresh breadcrumbs

½ cup / 20 g thyme leaves

Salt and freshly ground pepper

1 egg, beaten

1 piece pork belly, about 3 lb / 1.2 kg skin removed

Method

Prep and cook time: 3 h

1 Heat the oven to 400F (200 C / Gas Mark 6).

2 Heat the oil in a skillet and gently fry the onion until soft. Add the garlic and the chilies and cook for 2 more minutes. Stir in half the pine nuts, remove from the heat and transfer to a large bowl.

3 Stir in the breadcrumbs and half the thyme leaves and season with salt and pepper. Mix in the beaten egg.

4 Lay the pork flesh side up on a board and place the stuffing along its length. Roll up and secure with kitchen twine.

5 Score the meat with a sharp knife and rub with a little oil, salt and pepper. Transfer the meat to a roasting pan, cover with kitchen foil and roast for 30 minutes.

6 Turn the oven down to 350F (180C / Gas Mark 4) and roast for a further 1½ hours, basting every 20 minutes.

7 Remove the foil, turn the oven up to 425F (220C / Gas Mark 7), scatter the meat with the remaining pine nuts and thyme and return to the oven for 30 minutes.

8 Let the meat rest in a warm place for 15 minutes before serving.

BACON-WRAPPED TURKEY BREAST WITH ROOT VEGETABLES

Ingredients

3 tbsp grain mustard

2 tbsp honey

1 tsp paprika

Salt and freshly ground pepper

1 boned rolled turkey breast, about
3 lb / 1.2 kg

12 slices bacon

6 bay leaves

8 small carrots, peeled

8 small parsnips, peeled

1²/₃ cups / 400 ml chicken broth
(stock)

Method

Prep and cook time: 1 h 45 min

1 Heat the oven to 350F (180C / Gas Mark 4).

2 Mix together the mustard, honey and paprika.
Season with salt and pepper and rub all over the
turkey breast.

3 Wrap the turkey breast with the bacon and
secure with kitchen twine. Place the turkey breast
in a large roasting pan and tuck the bay leaves under
the twine.

4 Put the carrots and parsnips around the meat
and pour over the chicken broth (stock). Cover with
kitchen foil and roast in the oven for 1 hour, basting
every 20 minutes.

5 Remove the foil, turn the oven up to 425F (220C
Gas Mark 7) and roast for a further 15 minutes.

6 Let the meat rest for 15 minutes before serving.

ROAST CHICKEN LEG WITH HERBS

Ingredients

4 tbsp / 50 g butter, softened

2 tbsp Dijon mustard

Juice of 1 lemon

Salt and freshly ground pepper

4 chicken legs

2 tbsp vegetable oil

4 sprigs thyme

4 sprigs tarragon

20 sage leaves

1 cup / 250 ml chicken broth (stock)

1 tbsp honey

Boiled potatoes, to serve

Method

Prep and cook time: 40 min plus 1 h to marinate

1 Mix the butter with the mustard and lemon juice. Season with salt and pepper and smear all over the chicken legs. Set aside to marinate for 1 hour.

2 Heat the oven to 400F (200C / Gas Mark 6).

3 Heat the oil in a large ovenproof skillet and fry the chicken legs on all sides until just browned. Transfer the skillet to the oven and roast for about 40 minutes, basting occasionally, until the chicken is thoroughly cooked.

4 Remove the chicken legs from the skillet and keep warm. Put the skillet back on the heat, add the herbs and pour over the chicken broth (stock). Bring to a boil, stir in the honey and season with salt and pepper. Simmer for 5 minutes.

5 Serve the chicken legs with the sauce and herbs poured over and boiled potatoes alongside.

ROAST LAMB WITH INDIAN SPICES

Ingredients

1 small leg of lamb

2 tsp coriander seeds

2 tbsp cumin seeds

1 onion, roughly chopped

²/₃ cup / 50 g flaked almonds

2 garlic cloves

Thumb-size piece of fresh ginger, peeled and grated

2 green chilies, deseeded and chopped

2 tsp salt

2 cups / 500 ml yogurt

2 tbsp vegetable oil

1 tsp ground curcuma (turmeric)

1 tsp cayenne pepper

1 tsp garam masala

3 strips cassia bark

Method

Prep and cook time: 2 h plus 24 h to marinate

1 Score the skin of the lamb with a sharp knife

2 Toast the coriander and cumin seeds in a dry skillet until lightly browned then grind to a powder with a pestle and mortar.

3 Put the ground seeds, onion, almonds, garlic, ginger, chilies and salt into a food processor with 3 tbsp yogurt and blend to make a paste.

4 Heat the oil in a skillet and gently fry the curcuma (turmeric), cayenne and garam masala for 2 minutes. Stir in the paste and add the rest of the yogurt. Rub the mixture all over the lamb, cover and marinate in the refrigerator for 24 hours.

5 Remove the meat from the refrigerator 1 hour before you want to cook it. Heat the oven to 400F (200C / Gas Mark 6).

6 Transfer the lamb to a roasting pan and spread all the yogurt marinade over it. Tuck the cassia bark under the meat, cover with kitchen foil and roast for 1 hour.

7 Remove the foil, baste and cook a further 30 minutes. Let the meat rest for 15 minutes before serving.

ROAST POTATOES

Ingredients

2 lb / 800 g potatoes, peeled and halved

½ cup / 125 ml sunflower oil

Salt and freshly ground pepper

Method

Prep and cook time: 50 min

1 Preheat the oven to 425F (220C / Gas Mark 7).

2 Put the potatoes in a large pan of salted water and bring to a boil. Boil for 5 minutes then drain well. Return the potatoes to the pan and shake hard with the lid on to roughen the surface of the potatoes.

3 While the potatoes are boiling, put the oil into an ovenproof dish and heat in the oven.

4 Carefully add the drained and shaken potatoes to the hot oil and season with salt and pepper. Return the dish to the oven.

5 Roast for 35 minutes, turning once, or until the potatoes are golden brown.

NUT ROAST WITH CRANBERRIES, SPINACH AND GOAT CHEESE

Ingredients

1 cup /150 g cashew nuts

1 cup /150 g hazelnuts

1 cup / 125 g chestnuts, ready cooked and peeled

3 tbsp sunflower oil

2 onions, finely chopped

2 stalks celery, finely chopped

2 garlic cloves, finely chopped

2 cups / 100 g fresh breadcrumbs

1 cup / 100 g cranberries

20 sage leaves, chopped

2 sprigs thyme, chopped

4 sprigs parsley, chopped

Salt and freshly ground pepper

Juice of 1 lemon

2 eggs, beaten

8 oz / 200 g spinach

8 oz / 200 g goat cheese

Method

Prep and cook time: 1 h 20 min

1 Heat the oven to 350F (180C / Gas Mark 4).

2 Put the cashew nuts, hazelnuts and chestnuts into a dry skillet and toast over a moderate heat until the nuts are lightly browned.

3 Put the nuts in a food processor and pulse to coarsely chop them.

4 Heat the oil in the skillet and gently cook the onion and celery until soft. Add the garlic, cook for 2 more minutes then stir in the breadcrumbs and remove the pan from the heat.

5 Put the onion mixture into a large bowl and add the nuts, cranberries and herbs. Season with salt and pepper and stir in the lemon juice and the eggs.

6 Cook the spinach until wilted then drain and squeeze out any excess liquid.

7 Grease a 450 g / 1 lb loaf tin and spoon in half the nut mixture, pressing it down with the back of a spoon. Place the spinach on top of the nut mixture in the tin in a neat layer. Spread or slice the goat cheese over the spinach then add the rest of the nut mixture.

8 Pack the mixture down firmly then bake for 30–40 minutes. Let the loaf cool a little before turning out.

ROLLED STUFFED PORK BELLY

Ingredients

5 tbsp olive oil

1 small onion, chopped

1 red chili pepper, deseeded and finely chopped

1 tsp fennel seeds

2 cups / 100 g fresh breadcrumbs

1 tbsp chopped parsley

1 tbsp chopped sage

1 egg, beaten

Salt and freshly ground pepper

3 lb / 1.2 kg pork belly, boned

Method

Prep and cook time: 2 h

1 Heat the oven to 350F (180C / Gas Mark 4).

2 Heat 3 tbsp oil in a pan and gently fry the onion until soft. Add the chopped chili and fennel seeds, cook for 2 minutes then mix into the breadcrumbs with the parsley, sage and beaten egg. Season with salt and pepper.

3 Lay the pork flesh side up on a board and place the stuffing along the middle of the meat. Roll up tightly and secure with kitchen string.

4 Heat the remaining oil in a roasting pan and sear the pork all over until lightly browned.

5 Season the meat with salt and pepper and roast in the oven for 1¾ hours or until the juices from the meat run clear. Baste the meat every 30 minutes.

6 Let the meat rest for 15 minutes before slicing to serve.

TURBOT WITH CARROTS AND POTATOES

Ingredients

8 tbsp olive oil

2 large shallots, peeled and sliced vertically

½ celery stalk, chopped

2 carrots, chopped

2 large potatoes, peeled and finely sliced

Salt and freshly ground pepper

4 pieces turbot fillet, skin on

1 cup / 250 ml white wine

1 garlic clove, chopped

Juice of 1 lemon

2 tbsp chopped parsley

1 cup / 100 g black olives

Rosemary, to garnish

Method

Prep and cook time: 40 min

1 Heat the oven to 400F (200 C / Gas Mark 6).

2 Heat half the oil in a large skillet and cook the shallots and celery until soft. Add the carrots and potatoes, stir to coat all the vegetables with oil and season with salt and pepper. Transfer to an ovenproof dish and set the skillet aside.

3 Rub the turbot with a little oil, place on top of the vegetables skin side up and pour over the wine. Cover with kitchen foil and roast for about 20 minutes or until the fish is cooked through, basting after 10 minutes

4 When the fish is nearly cooked, heat the remaining oil in the skillet and gently fry the garlic for 1 minute. Add the lemon juice and a splash of water then stir in the parsley and olives.

5 Transfer the fish and vegetables to warmed serving plates and pour over the garlic, parsley and olives. Sprinkle with rock salt and serve immediately garnished with the rosemary.

Published by Transatlantic Press

First published in 2011

Transatlantic Press
38 Copthorne Road, Croxley Green, Hertfordshire WD3 4AQ

© Transatlantic Press

Images and Recipes by StockFood © The Food Image Agency

Recipes selected by Jonnie Léger, StockFood

A catalogue record for this book is available from the British Library.

ISBN 978-1-907176-91-3

Printed in China